MORE WESSEX WALKIES
for you and your dog

Dedicated to Joan Loader and my dog
Bounty for their assistance

Patricia M Wilnecker
1994

By the same author:

non-fiction
High Street Murders 1598
Published by Poole Museum Service
A History of Upper Parkstone (beginning to 1939)
Upper Parkstone in the Second World War
More Recollections of Old Upper Parkstone
Bounty, the tale of a dog
Wessex Walkies for you and your dog
Published by Patricia M Wilnecker

fiction:
The Bountifull Gyfte
Published by Patricia M Wilnecker

Published by Patricia M Wilnecker
73 Gwynne Road
Parkstone
Poole
Dorset
BH12 2AR

First published 1994
© P M Wilnecker

British Library Cataloguing in Publication Data
A catalogue record for this book is available from the British Library

ISBN 0 9513971 6 8

Typeset in Palatino 10/11 and printed in Great Britain by The Local History Press,
3 Devonshire Promenade, Lenton, Nottingham NG7 2DS.

CONTENTS

A map showing the locations of the walks can be found on pages 16 & 17.

continued overleaf...

Dog-permitted places of interest

INTRODUCTION

My first *Wessex Walkies* book was fun to write but this was even more so, as many of the walks were new to me too. Again, these are mainly 'suggested locations' so an Ordnance Survey map is recommended for the longer walks.

At the risk of 'preaching to the converted', I must again ask that dogs are kept under control in the vicinity of livestock, both for its safety and for that of your dog. I also hope it goes without saying that you will not allow your dog to foul footpaths or beaches - it gives our chums a bad reputation - and WE are to blame. Caution too, as there are adders in Wessex. If by mischance your dog is bitten, get him to a vet at once. Fortunately, if treated promptly bites are seldom fatal.

Having said all that, I hope you will enjoy these walks as much as we and the folks we met along the way did. Isn't it great how doggy people stop and chat? It's a fine way to make new friends!

NB. Where pubs and eating places are listed they are not necessarily starting points for the walks, but are conveniently near by car and will all accomodate dogs in one way or another. By 'dogs allowed outside only' this usually means in the pub gardens, where there are picnic tables.

DOG PERMITTED BEACHES
All year round:
 Mudeford Sandspit
 Hengistbury Head end of Southbourne
 East of Branksome Chine for a short distance
 West end of Sandbanks Pavilion
 Shell Bay (lead restrictions apply)
 Hamworthy
 Rockley
 Kimmeridge (rocky beach)
 Ringstead
 Weymouth (designated sections)

Most other beaches - dogs allowed on Promenade on lead.

WINTER - no restrictions

The walks in this book were all correct at the time of going to print, but places are liable to change. If you come across any of these or have favourite walks in Wessex suitable for dogs, please let me know - and thank you to those who did so and which I have included in this book.

Here's wishing you more happy walkies!

WALK 1   LYMINGTON SALTERNS

DURATION: *Flexible*
STARTING POINT: *Westfield Road, Lymington*
FOOD: *The Mayflower, Kings Saltern Road. Dogs allowed on lead.*

Cross the road to Lymington Yacht Haven boatyard and take the public footpath waymarked along the left hand side. Follow the signs and you emerge on to the Salterns, old pools which with natural evaporation formed salt and where the mineral was collected in bygone days. The path continues along the sea wall and if you wish you can follow it to Oxey Marsh and as far as Keyhaven. There are fine views of the Isle of Wight and the Hampshire coast. A good, bracing walk.

WALK 2   BANK, NEW FOREST

DURATION: *Flexible*
STARTING POINT: *Royal Oak, Bank, near Lyndhurst*
FOOD: *Royal Oak. Dogs welcome.*

Not far from the busy A35 but easily overlooked, Bank is signposted just outside Lyndhurst on the western (Bournemouth) side. From the far end of the tiny settlement - it is too small to be called a village - tracks lead into unspoilt forest. You may explore Hartshill Enclosure, Queens Meadow Wildlife Conservation Area and follow meandering small streams, one of which forms the upper reaches of Lymington River. Deer live here, as in many parts of the New Forest but please restrain your dog from chasing these gentle creatures. It can be boggy in places so sturdy footwear is essential.

WALK 3   RHINEFIELD ORNAMENTAL DRIVE, NEW FOREST

DURATION: *Flexible*
STARTING POINT: *Car park, Ornamental Drive.*
FOOD: *Foresters Arms, Brookley Road, Brockenhurst. Dogs allowed in public bar.*

The Ornamental Drive crosses the A35 roughly halfway between Christchurch and Lyndhurst. You want the one on the right, coming from Christchurch which is signposted. Drive along this narrow road with passing places, past the right angled corner. Shortly, on your right you will see the mansion of Rhinefield, now a hotel. I have seen this silhouetted against the sky at night during a thunderstorm and it can look like Dracula's Castle!

There are several car parks off the road as you go along the Ornamental Drive - so called because of the specimen trees which grow there - but to my mind the one as you emerge on to the heath after the trees on the left has the most to offer. It follows a pretty, gravel-bedded stream (the Ober Water) and is waymarked with coloured posts. If you continue up the hill to the grassy/heather open ground there are even toilets! This is a pleasant walk at any time of the year.

WALK 4   BARTON ON SEA COASTAL PATH
DURATION: *Flexible*
STARTING POINT: *Car park, east end of Marine Drive, Barton on Sea.*
FOOD: *Beachcomber Restaurant, Marine Drive. Open all year. Dogs welcome on a lead.*

The coastal path runs between the cliff top and the golf club, giving superb views across to the Isle of Wight with the Needles, Tennyson Down and the northern part of the island clearly visible. It is possible to follow the path as far as Milford on Sea, a distance of several miles, before encountering traffic. Westwards from your starting point, the walk may be extended for another mile along the grassy cliff tops of Barton on Sea.

WALK 5   BROOK AVENUE, NEW MILTON
DURATION: *Short*
STARTING POINT: *Roadside in Brook Avenue*

A short but pleasant walk, this will take you through trees and grass with a small stream running through the centre. Wooden seats are placed strategically along the way so you may sit and contemplate nature and watch your dog sniffing happily off the lead.

WALK 6   CHEWTON BUNNY
DURATION: *Short*
STARTING POINT: *Mill Lane, Highcliffe*

Footpath signs indicate the direction to follow. A hidden stream finds its way down to the sea through a wooded glen and an area of open grassland. Rabbits abound here at dusk. The walk may be extended out of season by following the sea shore in either direction. Tiny black shark's teeth, approximately 125 million years old and other fossils can often be found amongst gravel on the beach in this area.

WALK 7   HOLMSLEY
DURATION: *Flexible*
STARTING POINT: *Holmsley Walk car park*
FOOD: *The Cat and Fiddle Harvester Inn, Hinton Admiral. Dogs outside in large garden only.*

Take the turning off the A35 by the signpost that reads 'Godwinscroft 2 miles'. After about a quarter of a mile turn right into Forest Road and continue through the '40 mile zone' sign. This is a very straight road and was part of a three runway airfield, one of several in this area used in World War Two from 1941/46. As well as RAF, men from the US and Canadian Airforce were stationed here and Spitfires, Typhoons, Mustangs and B26's used this airfield. On the level hilltop runways can still be defined even though the surfaces have been demolished. All is peaceful now though, and there is a large, free car park by the entrance to Holmsley Camp Site. Downhill there are miles of really beautiful undulating broad leafed forest, bogs and streams. Before you have gone very far you may come across a holly wood - not the film variety but a wood consisting mainly of ancient hollies, giving shelter to the forest creatures, ponies, cattle and deer alike.

WALK 8   SPRING BUSHES, NEAR HIGH CORNER INN
DURATION: *Flexible*
STARTING POINT: *Spring Bushes car park, Moyles Court to Linwood Road*
FOOD: *High Corner Inn. Dogs welcome*
This is a narrow road with passing places. The turning to High Corner Inn - a rough track - is on your left while nearby on the right is Spring Bushes car park. A path leads into pinewoods and along grassy rides. If you keep turning right you will emerge in Ameys Wood just down the road from your starting place, or simply explore at will.

WALK 9   APPLESLADE, NEW FOREST
DURATION: *Shortish, but may be extended*
STARTING POINT: *Car park on opposite side of road near the Red Shoot Inn*
FOOD: *Red Shoot Inn. Dogs allowed in public bar*
From Moyles Court take the Linwood road and approximately 500 yards before the Red Shoot Inn on the right is a free car park, Appleslade. A short circular walk of about half an hour may be taken by following the path through the trees, or explore at will in the broad leafed woodland.

WALK 10 FURZE HILL, NORTH GORLEY
DURATION: *Flexible*
STARTING POINT: *Furze Hill*
FOOD: *Alice Lisle, Moyles Court*
From Ringwood take the Mockbeggar then North Gorley roads. When you reach a sign pointing right to Furze Hill, follow its direction until you reach a 'no through road'. Go along this. It soon degenerates into a gravel track then peters out. Park here considerately so as not to block the entrance to several cottages, then you can walk for miles! Gently undulating heathland hills roll away into the distance interspersed with the furze (local name for gorse) which gave the area its name. On a clear day there are fine views in all directions.

WALK 11 EYEWORTH POND, NEW FOREST
DURATION: *Flexible*
STARTING POINT: *Eyeworth Pond free car park*
FOOD: *Royal Oak, Fritham. Drinks and crisps only, but dogs welcome.*
From Stoney Cross go in the direction of Fritham. By an unusual towered building which is now the New Forest Nursing Home turn left into the road to 'Fritham and Eyeworth only'. Branch right into the 'no through road' past the Royal Oak Pub and continue to the very end of the tarmac road. Here you will discover Eyeworth Pond with its resident ducks - mallard, mandarin and white. A track runs alongside the lake through forest and heath where you may glimpse green woodpeckers and deer. The grass is cropped short by ponies and a small stream bubbles its way to join the lake. A very pleasant walk.

WALK 12 GODSHILL - ASHLEY WALK
DURATION: *Flexible*
STARTING POINT: *Ashley Walk car park and picnic place*
FOOD: *The Fighting Cocks, Godshill. Dogs welcome in public bar. A friendly pub.*
From Fordingbridge go past Sandy Balls Caravan Park on the Godshill road then past the Fighting Cocks Inn. On top of the hill park in the second large free car park on the right. A gravel track, known locally as the Snake Path winds down and up over the hills for a 'dry' walk. There are miles of tracks to explore freely, but waterproof footwear is essential if you leave the gravel track - and take care to avoid the bogs. This is lovely, rolling open heathland with New Forest ponies, sheep, cattle, rabbity scents and fine views. If you are new to the Forest do not be tempted to approach the ponies. They ARE wild and accidents can happen so keep your dog under control too.

WALK 13 SALISBURY TO OLD SARUM
DURATION: *2 miles each way*
STARTING POINT: *Main car park near Sainsbury's*
FOOD: *Old Castle Inn, Old Castle Road. Dogs allowed in garden.*
Follow the river upstream (parts of this walk are 'on the lead') to Stratford-sub-Castle. From there a footpath leads uphill to Old Sarum, the 56 acre site of the original Salisbury Cathedral and described in that fine saga 'Sarum', by Edward Rutherford. Old Sarum was first an Iron Age hill fort. Later it was occupied in succession by Romans, Saxons and finally the Normans who built the castle, cathedral and Bishops Palace.

There are superb views from the ramparts with the rivers Avon, Bourne and Nadder below you encompassing the fine cathedral with its unmistakable tall spire.

When you have had your fill of the view, grassy earthworks and wooded slopes are there for you to explore before returning by the same route.

WALK 14 TIDPIT DOWN

DURATION: *Flexible*
STARTING POINT: *Small car park up a track on Cranborne/Martin road*
FOOD: *Fleur de Lys, Cranborne. Dogs welcome*

As you drive downhill towards Martin you will see grassy downland on your left. A rough track leads up to the small car park. Leaving your car, climb uphill, pausing to enjoy the view towards Martin Down, Rockbourne and West Park with its Roman Villa, when you reach the crest. The land here is private but the owner allows walkers and horse riders to use it 'for their pleasure' -how kind in this day and age. If you would like a longer walk you may continue to Martin Down, described in my first *Wessex Walkies* book.

WALK 15 BOTTLEBUSH ROMAN ROAD

DURATION: *Flexible*
STARTING POINT: *Bottlebush Down on the B3081*
FOOD: *The Coote Arms, on the A354 Blandford/Shaftesbury Road. Dogs welcome.*

Two parallel banks extend in both directions from the B3081 at Bottlebush Down near the junction with the A354 at Handley Cross. What were their origins? Some say they were connected with the Dorset Cursus which may have been a Roman racecourse or a prehistoric ceremonial route - there are ancient tumuli nearby so this could well be so. Be that as it may, it is beautiful walking country and if one encounters spirits from the past - all the more exciting!

The longest walk is westward. Simply follow the banks, even though the path veers off to the left after about half a mile.

To the east you can see the Roman road stretching out straight as an arrow until it joins with the modern road to Salisbury. This, too is a pleasant walk alongside a field and by a wood with rolling open countryside all around.

WALK 16 KNOWLTON RINGS

DURATION: *Short*
STARTING POINT: *Layby off the B3078 Wimborne/Cranborne road*

From the B3078 Wimborne to Cranborne road take the turning left to Brockington/Wimborne St Giles and you will find Knowlton Rings just off the main road on your right. Although only a short walk it can be a good 'leg stretcher' on the way to somewhere else or a pleasant place for a picnic. A single rampart and ditch enclose a ruined church which was abandoned after the Black Death of 1348 when the population of Knowlton village was wiped out. Ancient burial barrows are scattered around the area and the 'Rings' reputedly date back to the Bronze Age. Wild flowers and butterflies can be found here in profusion in Summer months.

WALK 17 EDMONDSHAM TO CRANBORNE AND RETURN

DURATION: *Approx 1 hour each way*
STARTING POINT: *The old pump, Edmondsham*
FOOD: *The Fleur de Lys, Cranborne. Well-behaved dogs allowed*

Coming from Wimborne on the B3078, after approximately 9 miles take the turning on the right to Edmondsham. When you reach Edmondsham House turn right again and follow the boundary hedge and fences and then the road to Cripplestyle for a short distance until you reach a roofed water pump dated 1884. Park here in the small layby and follow the straight gravel track alongside it. Fork left at the top of the rise and continue through Edmonsham woods. There are rabbity scents for your dog, and you are in 'deepest Dorset', far from the holiday makers trails. When fields and open country come in sight through the trees bear left. You will pass a huge pit with an ancient yew tree growing in it on the far side along the way on your left. On a hill in the woods are ditches and banks, the only remnants of a motte and bailey castle. As Cranborne comes in sight you should find a short cut over a stile on the right. This crosses a field, emerging into Castle Street. Food or coffee is available at the Fleur de Lys and it is worth exploring the quiet village of Cranborne (once the main village of the Royal Hunting Ground of Cranborne Chase) before you leave. After rain, parts of this walk can be very muddy.

There is a Garden Centre nearby but they do not admit dogs.

WALK 18 ASHLEY HEATH

DURATION: *Flexible*
STARTING POINT: *Layby opposite St Ives Park (cul de sac) or 100 yards further on towards Ringwood*
FOOD: *Frampton Mill, Furlong Centre, Ringwood. Dogs outside only but in a pleasant pedestrianised area by a life-like bronze of a New Forest mare and foal; or The Old Taps, Station Road, West Moors. Dogs allowed on a lead.*

From Ashley Heath roundabout take the Moors Valley road. Approximately a quarter of a mile on the left is a cul de sac called St Ives Park. Immediately opposite is a layby with free parking and a sign, 'Forestry Commission, no horse riding'. This is an area of predominately pinewoods abounding with squirrels. There are many wide paths to choose from and also narrower ones, but these can be rather brambly with muddy patches.

Ashley Heath is in the Guinness Book of Records as having the smallest High Street in the country - four shops! Above them is a small spire, a clock and the cryptic inscription, 'The night cometh'.

WALK 19 MATCHAMS PARK, HURN FOREST (NOT the Stadium)

DURATION: *Flexible*
STARTING POINT: *Matchams Lane*
FOOD: *Catherine Wheel, St Catherines Hill*

Coming from the direction of Bournemouth, drive along Matchams Lane past the end of Hurn Airport's runway with its 'fairy lights'. After a quarter of a mile on the left hand side is a car park with a sign 'Matchams Park car park'. Pinewoods and heath stretch as far as the eye can see with many paths radiating star-like from the main gravel track. Lovely and safe for your dog - but mind YOU don't get lost!

WALK 20 RAMSDOWN

DURATION: *Flexible*
STARTING POINT: *Avon Causway Road from Hurn Bridge. Car park by Christchurch Sporting Club*
FOOD: *Catherine Wheel, St Catherines Hill. Dogs allowed in public bar*

A wide path with the remains of a tarmac surface leads from the car park. Keep straight on along this path which will take you to the top of the hill after about 15 minutes. From the flat plateau, if the weather is clear, you will have unsurpassed views to the far horizons in all directions. The 'polar bear' at the Needles in the Isle of Wight is visible and Bournemouth's Hurn Airport is below you while from the south side of the plateau the old house in the trees is Hurn Court, formerly the home of Lord Malmesbury and now a school. A walk not to be missed.

WALK 21 IFORD BRIDGE RECREATION GROUND

DURATION: *Short*
STARTING POINT: *Old Bridge Road*
FOOD: *Kelly's Kitchen, Christchurch High Street. 'No Dogs' sign on door, but they are allowed in the pretty walled garden at the rear.*

Cross over the bridge and you will discover an open grassy area alongside the riverbank. Swans and ducks compete with each other for food and in Spring may often be seen nesting in reeds by the water. A pleasant walk.

WALK 22 IFORD BRIDGE, UPSTREAM

DURATION: *Short*
STARTING POINT: *Bridle Crescent, Iford Bridge*

On the up-river side of Iford Bridge a sign reads 'Footpath to Holdenhurst'. Perhaps there was once, but about half-way along, a Throop Fisheries sign declares that the land is private property. Nevertheless it is a pleasant walk as far as it goes, following the grassy bank of the Stour with trees on the inland side and quite safe 'off the lead'. On the opposite side of the river is a golf course. The footpath can be rather 'squidgy' after rain, so take care.

WALK 23 BOSCOMBE CLIFFS
DURATION: *Extent of walk one mile*
STARTING POINT: *Boscombe Overcliff Drive*
From the Marina/Grove Road, Boscombe a footpath leads through clifftop gardens where squirrels and pigeons abound. On leaving the trees you emerge on to grassy, windswept cliffs scattered with gorse bushes. There is a tarmac path if the weather has been wet and the cliffs are safely fenced. Views extend over Poole Bay to the Purbeck Hills, Swanage and the Needles off the Isle of Wight. Locals call the white cliff behind the Needles the 'Polar Bear' which can easily be identified on this walk. You can continue along the cliffs as far as Southbourne.

WALK 24 KINGS PARK, BOSCOMBE
DURATION: *Short*
STARTING POINT: *Harewood Avenue*
The grassy park stretches uphill towards the football ground which is home to AFC Bournemouth. At the Harewood Avenue end - site of the ancient Thistle Barrow - the terrain is rougher but pleasant for a short, safe walk.

WALK 25 DUDSBURY
DURATION: *Short*
STARTING PLACE: *Park near Bridge House, Longham*
A footpath runs between a wooden fence and the Bridge House car park then widens out on to the grassy riverbank. Follow this winding path, then climb uphill to Dudsbury, once an Iron Age Camp but now one for Girl Guides! Pleasant walking with a steep-ish climb but there are plans to improve this with steps.

WALK 26 CHURCH FARM RIVER WALK, WEST PARLEY
DURATION: *Approximately half an hour, round trip*
STARTING POINT: *Far end of Church Lane*
From Parley Cross take the Hurn road then turn first right into Church Lane. Drive to the end and park considerately in the road near the tiny church of All Saints which dates back to Saxon times and is well worth a visit. Unlike most churches its layout is not east-west but faces sunrise on All Saints Day as it was prior to 1752. Half way between the churchyard gate and the church door on the right is a

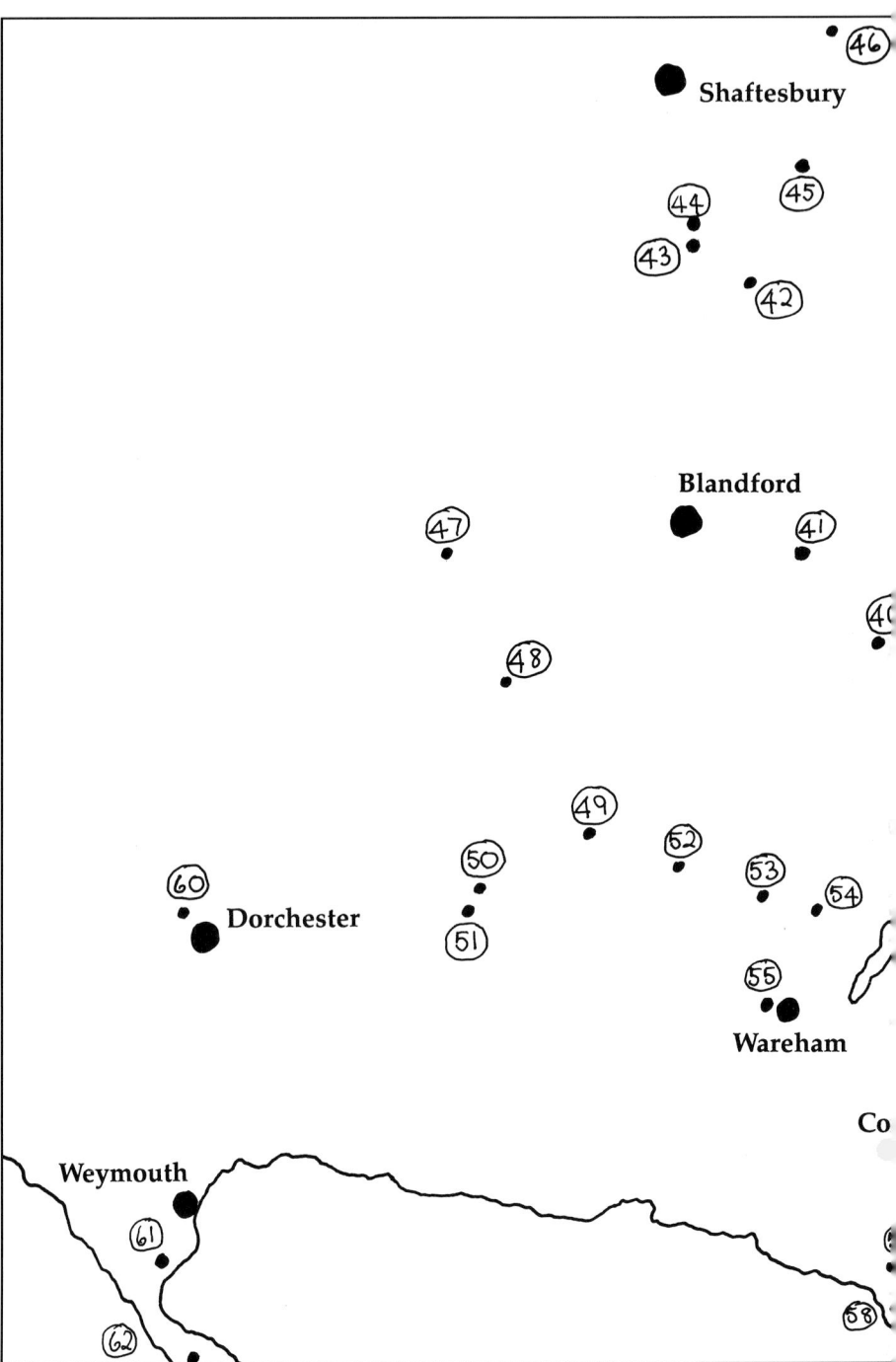

Shaftesbury

Blandford

Dorchester

Wareham

Weymouth

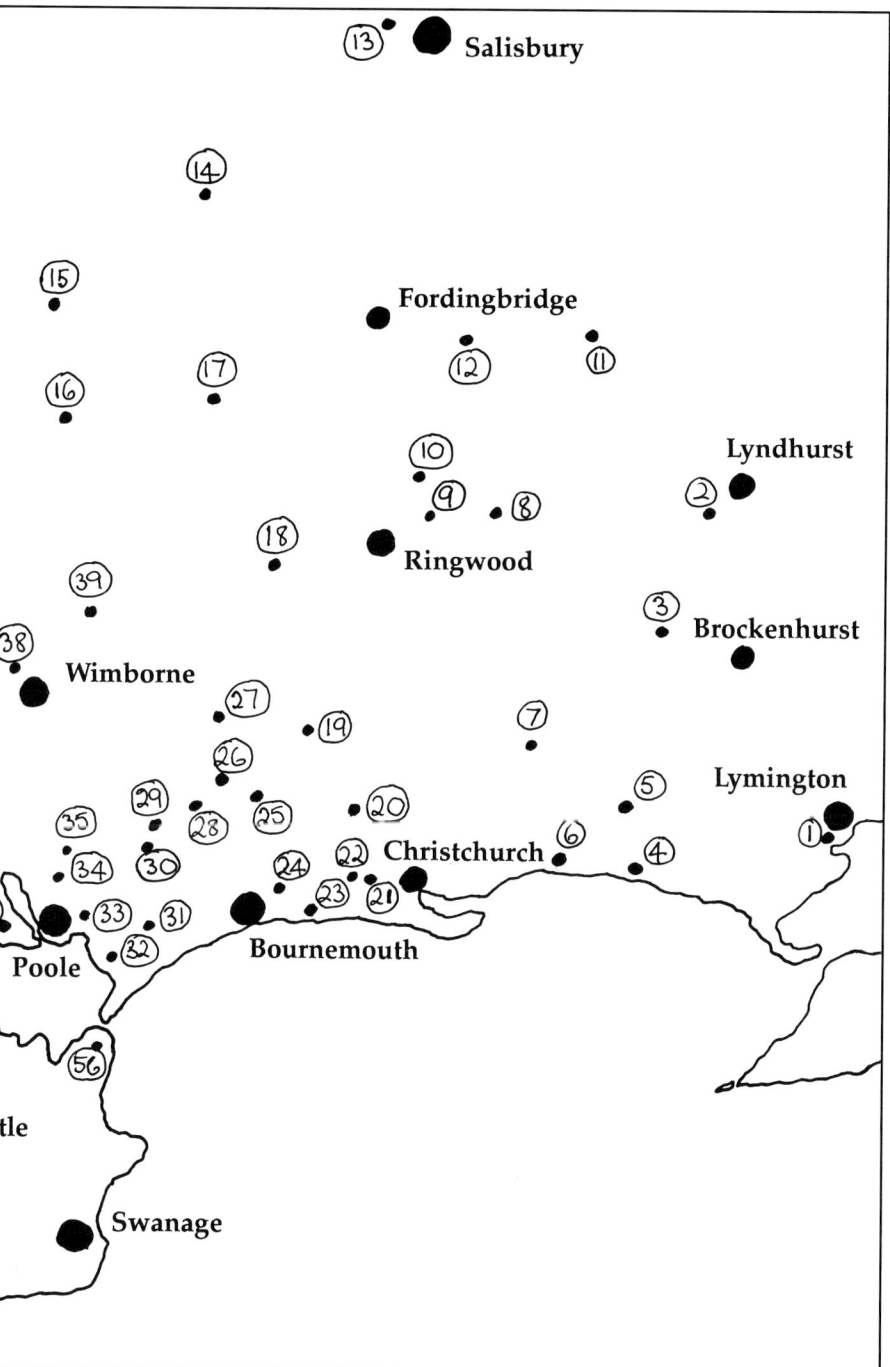

Salisbury

Fordingbridge

Lyndhurst

Ringwood

Brockenhurst

Wimborne

Lymington

Christchurch

Bournemouth

Poole

stle

Swanage

sundial, set on part of the old gibbet where felons were hanged. According to legend, due to its horrific past the sundial never tells the correct time.

The walk begins through a farm gate and follows a short avenue of leylandii, thence along the river bank.

WALK 27 PARLEY COMMON
DURATION: *Flexible*
STARTING POINT: *Lone Pine Drive, Off New Road*
Off Lone Pine Close, at the right angle with Lone Pine Drive is a footpath leading on to Parley Common. This is heather, gorse and bracken country and although not as hilly as some of the other walks the air can be very invigorating.

WALK 28 NEW ROAD, WATER LANE FARM
DURATION: *Flexible*
STARTING POINT: *Bournemouth end of New Road by the Roundabout*
A cul de sac leads off the roundabout and to the Sewage Works - but do not let this put you off or you will miss a lovely walk!

Leave your car in the cul de sac and follow the sign pointing to Cherry Tree Nursery. There are views across the river to West Parley with its tiny church (see West Parley Church walk) as well as grassy paths encompassing wide open tracts of land to explore. If you follow the river downstream you will eventually reach Muscliffe, described in my first *Wessex Walkies* book.

WALK 29 EAST HOWE COMMON
DURATION: *Shortish/flexible*
STARTING POINT: *Kinson Swimming Baths*
A path runs along the rear of the baths through woodland and thence to a grassy area. A bit muddy in places (there is a stream) but an oasis in a built-up area for an off the lead walk.

WALK 30 TURBARY COMMON
DURATION: *Flexible*
STARTING POINT: *Turbary Park Avenue, between Kinson Road, Wallisdown and Poole Lane.*
Another pocket of heathland hidden away in a town and extending further than would at first appear, the Common is best reached from Turbary Park Avenue approximately 200 yards past the junction with Fernheath Avenue, travelling west. A five bar gate on your left is adjacent to a sign marked 'Turbary Common' and

stating that this is an area of Special Scientific Interest. To the east is a low area of marshy ground and trees, while to the west in September 1993 I discovered about an acre of teazle growing as closely as wheat in a cornfield. I have never before seen teazle growing as thickly or as widespread as this. There were also great clumps of golden rod, wild asters and rosebay willow, as well as the usual gorse and heather. From the highest point distant horizons can be seen including Hurn Airport. The name 'Turbary' means the right of commoners to dig turf. There are many paths to explore, and it is safe, off the lead territory for your dog.

WALK 31 ALDER HILLS NATURE RESERVE
DURATION: *Short*
STARTING POINT: *Sharp Road, close to the Dorset Knob Pub*

A secret lake hidden away behind a small industrial estate is a 13 acre wild life haven created from an old flooded claypit used by Sharp Jones Pottery and now managed by the Dorset Trust for Nature Conservation. A rough track winds through trees, heather, gorse and bracken and will take you right around the lake. The waters are clear but very deep and you will often see fishermen passing the days here in quiet solitude while dragon and damsel flies hover over the still surface.

Remember though, this is a scheduled Site of Special Scientific Interest so do not disturb the wild life, and please keep to the paths as heathland, especially on a slope such as this, erodes very easily.

WALK 32 EVENING HILL
DURATION: *Short*
STARTING POINT: *Evening Hill, Sandbanks Road*

You may park on the roadside or in winter in the small car park alongside the East Dorset Sailing Club. The lower part of the walk by the water is very suitable for wheelchairs and there are several seats as well. This is a beautiful way to spend a tranquil summer's evening with the gentle slap of the waves and the distant phut-phut of motor boats. The view over the harbour is one of my favourites. The more agile may climb steps at the western end which lead to a natural grass and tree area on top of the hill with even better views across the harbour. Short, but very sweet!

WALK 33 WHITECLIFF, POOLE
DURATION: *Short*
STARTING POINT: *Car park, junction of Sandbanks Road/Whitecliff Road*

This is a wide, grassy expanse of doggy paradise overlooking Parkstone Bay, part of Poole Harbour. The walk can be extended to the west as far as Poole Quay by following the shoreline path and to the east of the grassy area into Turks Lane which takes you past a boatyard and yacht club to a tiny beach on Parkstone Lake, with fine views over the harbour and Purbeck Hills.

WALK 34 PARKSTONE HEIGHTS/DONKEY FIELD
DURATION: *Short*
STARTING POINT: *Constitution Hill section of Parkstone Heights cul-de-sac*
An old rough track continues from the end of Parkstone Heights into pinewoods which conceal the old site of the Russell-Cotes Barnardo's Home. The track passes below The Hermitage (which was once the home of Jesse Carter of Pottery fame) and emerges on to a grassy open space approximately where the old 'Donkey Field' used to be and where many Poole youngsters did their courting in days gone by - and possibly still do! There is a seat from which to admire the fine views across Poole Harbour to Corfe Castle and the surrounding areas.

WALK 35 ST GEORGE'S CHURCH OAKDALE TO CANFORD HEATH
DURATION: *Flexible*
STARTING POINT: *Darbys Lane, near St George's Church, Oakdale*
FOOD: *Stepping Stones Inn, 180 The Broadway, Broadstone. Dogs allowed in public bar.*
Park at the 'blind' end of Darbys Lane and go over a footbridge which crosses the busy Old Wareham Road. You will then see a track which passes between the Nuffield Industrial Estate and a school playing field and which you should follow. In centuries past, this was Long Flette, not the area known as Longfleet today and to quote the 'Greate Boke of Poole' of 1567 was where 'The herde be driven owte of the towne by the kowards toords the Loge of Canfford pasturying by the way...in the north Syd of redd sand and so to the moore... refresssing them sellfis in the hete of the Daye in the somr tyme....'

Just before the Lodge on the right (which has a notice on the gate, 'Beware - patrolling rabbits'!) a path leads off to woods and grassy parkland and looks rather inviting. If you want a longer walk, however, do not be distracted but continue on past the Lodge where a tarmac path, safely fenced, skirts the Industrial Estate on the left. This was the site of the lake where the 'herdes refressed them sellfis' but has now been drained. An underpass takes you beneath Canford Heath Road and on to a newish red brick path which continues for a good half mile (it must have cost a fortune!) and then on to Canford Heath, where to the north the 'redd sand' can still be seen.

Although Dorset Heathland is said to be disappearing there are still miles of it ahead of you to explore.

WALK 36 HAMWORTHY PARK
DURATION: *Short*
STARTING POINT: *Car park in Lulworth Avenue*
FOOD: *The Park Café snack bar has tables outside in fine weather*
A wide expanse of grass, a dog-permitted beach all year round, views across to the beautiful islands of Poole Harbour and the Purbeck Hills beyond - what more could you want? Easily passed by on the nearby busy Blandford Road, this walk should NOT be missed. Bounty loves it!

WALK 37 ROMAN ROAD, UPTON
DURATION: *Flexible*
STARTING POINT: *Car park, Upton House*
FOOD: *Upton House Cafeteria, dogs outside on patio only.*
From Upton House car park follow the Castleman Trail signs inland, crossing Upton Road via the underpass to Longmeadow Lane. The footpath is waymarked on your left and could take you to Corfe Hills, Broadstone, but there are many tempting paths leading on to the heath or off through the woods inviting you to explore. The old road led from the Roman port at Hamworthy to Badbury Rings where there was a camp.

WALK 38 WALFORD MILL TO WIMBORNE VIA RIVER ALLEN
DURATION: *Short*
STARTING POINT: *Walford Mill Craft Centre and Cafe car park*
FOOD: *Walford Mill, dogs outside only*
Cross over the main road and follow the footpath sign downstream alongside Tice's Garage. This is quite safe off the lead and you may discover a peaceful backwater you didn't know existed. The footpath passes a school playing field then crosses a bridge, emerging by the large Allenview car park. If you continue along the banks of the river you will reach the centre of Wimborne.

WALK 39 WHITESHEET HILL
DURATION: *Flexible*
STARTING POINT: *Car park in clump of fir trees on Higher Row to Wimborne road*
FOOD: *Old Inn, Holt. Dogs outside only, or a bit further afield, Old Taps Inn, and the Elephant and Castle, Station Road, West Moors. Dogs allowed on a lead.*
One of the largest lowland heaths left in Dorset, the approximately 2000 acres of wide open spaces are worth exploring. Here you will find heather and gorse, with

rarer species if you search hard enough as this is a National Nature Reserve. There are fine views to the Isle of Wight, New Forest and the skyline of Bournemouth. Cautionary note, though - the paths can be very boggy.

WALK 40 HERON DROVE, BADBURY RINGS
DURATION: *Flexible*
STARTING POINT: *Wimborne-Blandford road, car park opposite sign to Sturminster Marshall*
FOOD: *True Lovers Knot, Tarrant Keynston. Well-behaved dogs on lead welcome*
Follow the footpath signs along the track which leads uphill. You have a choice of skirting the wood, leaving it on your left and following the path back to the road near Lodge Farm or going straight on passing Badbury Rings on your left and the wood (which is private) on your right. Lodge Farm was a late 14th century Medieval Hunting Lodge, possibly built for John of Gaunt. The footpaths trace the site of the old 300 acre deer park.

WALK 41 BUZBURY RINGS
DISTANCE: *approx 1 mile each way*
STARTING POINT: *Layby on RHS of road alongside True Lovers Knot, Tarrant Keynston*
FOOD: *True Lovers Knot, Tarrant Keynston. Well-behaved dogs on a lead welcome*
The layby is next to a ford opposite the first hedge on the left going uphill. A fingerboard sign reads 'Buzbury Rings 1' and points along a grassy track hedged on either side. This is rural Dorset, with pheasants squawking in the hedgerows and rabbits disappearing into their burrows. We have never actually reached Buzbury Rings - once a Celtic earthwork but now part of a golf course - as it is on the opposite side of the busy Wimborne to Blandford road but this does not detract from the walk in any way as the grassy track is very safe and pleasant in itself. This is one of Bounty's favourites.

WALK 42 WASHERS PIT
DURATION: *Flexible*
STARTING POINT: *Car park on south side of the Ashmore/Fontmell Magna road*
FOOD: *Compton Abbas Airfield. Dogs allowed in patio dining area*
At the bottom of the hill where the road dips down from the picturesque village of Ashmore with its pond made famous by the 'moonrakers' you will see a small car park. A sign reads, 'Washers Pit', and various paths for you to explore lead through

this wooded valley. Washers Pit was a dark, lonely pond, once overhung by huge trees and reputedly haunted by a woman in white - so if your dog's hackles rise - beware!

WALK 43 FONTMELL DOWN
DURATION: *Flexible*
STARTING POINT: *Viewpoint, small free car park on the Blandford to Shaftesbury (top) road, approx 4 miles from Shaftesbury.*
FOOD: *Compton Abbas Airfield. Dogs allowed on patio dining area.*
A footpath leads along the crest of the hill straight ahead. To the right of the path is Clubmans Down, while at Fontmell Down traces of ancient field systems can still be seen. It is worthwhile consulting the information board at the viewpoint before you begin. Try to choose a clear day for this walk and you will be well rewarded by spectacular views.

WALK 44 MELBURY BEACON
DURATION: *Flexible*
STARTING POINT: *Viewpoint - small free car park on Blandford - Shaftesbury (top) road, approx 4 miles from Shaftesbury.*
FOOD: *Compton Abbas Airfield. Dogs allowed on patio dining area.*
A rough track with the sign 'unsuitable for motors' runs downhill from the viewpoint. In summer the verges are a mass of wild flowers and assorted butterflies, the most abundant I have seen. After a few hundred yards on the right there is a stile (National Trust) to Compton Down and Melbury Beacon. The views across the chalk downland and Blackmore Vale are superb, but remember to control your dog if there are animals in the fields.

On reaching Melbury Down you will see the remains of the Armada Beacon of 1588, part of a chain along the hilltops to warn of invasion by Spain. At the bottom of the valley is Melbury Abbas mill. Water powered, there has been a mill on this site since the Domesday Book. The chalk stream that supplies the power is the little River Sturke.

WALK 45 WINGREEN
DURATION: *Flexible*
STARTING POINT: *Wingreen car park, reached from the B3081 Sixpenny Handley to Shaftesbury road.*
FOOD: *Compton Abbas Airfield. Dogs allowed in patio dining area.*
One of the highest spots for miles, Wingreen with its clump of trees can be seen from as far away as Bournemouth. A rough track leads from the road to a large car

park with really superb views in all directions. If you walk past the clump of trees you will find a footpath which will take you eventually to Tollard Royal, winding along the crest of the hill. A lovely walk, with fine panoramic views.

WALK 46 OLD WARDOUR CASTLE
DURATION: *Flexible*
STARTING POINT: *Old Wardour Castle*
FOOD: *The Forester, Lower Street, Donhead. Well behaved dogs allowed lunchtimes.*
Reached from the A30 four and a half miles NE of Shaftesbury. Park at Old Wardour Castle which is a 14th century ruin by a picturesque lake, and take the path that leads uphill through woods behind the castle. When you emerge from the woods the path continues across a field then branches out, giving you several choices of direction.

The castle was badly damaged in 1643 by the Roundheads then landscaped in the 18th century. On your walk you pass under a bridge which was part of this landscaping. This is rural Wiltshire at its best.

WALK 47 BULBARROW
DURATION: *Short*
STARTING POINT: *Bulbarrow car park*
From the large viewpoint car park overlooking the Blackmore Vale head westwards, and where three roads meet follow the signpost to Mappowder and Stoke Wake. Almost immediately on your right are two entrances to a sloping grassy parking area which is very pleasant for a picnic. There are fine views - as far as Somerset on a clear day - and a short walk through the scrub and trees produces interesting rabbity scents for your dog.

If you would like a longer walk with really spectacular views, continue approximately a quarter of a mile along the road to Stoke Wake and you will see a waymarked footpath to Rawlsbury Camp, an Iron Age hill fort, on your left.

WALK 48 MILTON ABBAS
DURATION: *Flexible*
STARTING POINT: *Milton Abbey car park (charge)*
FOOD: *Milton Arms, Dorchester Hill, Winterborne Whitchurch. Dogs allowed in public bar.*
Walk away from Milton Abbey in the direction of Hilton. Just around the bend on the right a steep path leads up into woodland which extends for several miles and was the deer park of Lord Milton (builder of the 'new' village) in the mid 18th century.

The Milton Abbey Public School was Lord Milton's mansion and the parkland around it laid out by Capability Brown, the great landscape designer. Although part of the park has been turned into playing fields it is still a very beautiful setting.

A further walk can be taken by passing the playing fields and continuing towards Hilton. After a short distance on your left a bridle path leads down through trees and over a little stream into more extensive woodland.

WALK 49 BERE REGIS/BLACK HILL
DURATION: *Flexible*
STARTING POINT: *Bere Regis free car park*
FOOD: *Royal Oak, Bere Regis. Open all day. Dogs on a lead welcome in bar and garden.*

This is a gem of a walk! The car park adjoins Manor Farm Road and where it meets Elder Road and a grassy area by a stream there is a raised wooden walkway and a gravel path which wends its way through a pretty area alongside the clear brook. Follow it upstream until you reach the unfortunately named but very pretty village of Shitterton (sometimes modestly known as 'Sitterton'). Go over the bridge and follow the road for 100 yards or so then take the footpath alongside house number 13. This emerges into an ancient sunken footpath overhung with trees which climbs up to Black Hill, an area of rough common and part of Thomas Hardy's Egdon Heath where deer can sometimes be seen. There are wide grassy paths on the top, nibbled down by rabbits and fine views of Bere Regis village, Poole Harbour, Purbeck and Affpuddle Heath whilst hidden away on the summit is a working gravel pit.

An alternative walk is to follow the blue bridleway markers from the west end of Shitterton along a usually dry gravel track which again will take you to Black Hill.

These are both lovely quiet walks and well recommended if you do not already know them.

WALK 50 BRIANTSPUDDLE
DURATION: *Flexible*
STARTING POINT: *The War Memorial, Briantspuddle*
FOOD: *The Royal Oak, Bere Regis. Open all day. Dogs on a lead welcome in bar and garden.*

From Briantspuddle village take the Bladen Valley road. A couple of hundred yards on the left is a wide gravel area with a War Memorial. Park (considerately please!) here and follow the gravel road between the thatched cottages. Although these appear old, they were designed by a Swedish architect in 1914 for the philanthropist Sir Ernest Debenham of Debenham and Freebody fame and built by the villagers themselves.

At the top end is a footpath which will take you gently uphill to woods. Obscure notices some 12 feet up in trees state the path into the woods is private, but if you skirt the woods to the left it will take you to Briantspuddle village, whereas right leads eventually to the Weymouth road. There are bluebells here in Spring and squirrels abound at all times of the year. A pretty walk.

WALK 51 AFFPUDDLE HEATH
DURATION: *Flexible*
STARTING POINT: *Affpuddle Heath car park and picnic place, east off B3390 and 2 miles south of Affpuddle.*
FOOD: *Royal Oak, Bere Regis. Open all day. Dogs on lead welcome in bar and beer garden.*
The area by the picnic place is a mature pinewood forest. We prefer the bridle path on the opposite side of the main road (follow the blue arrows) which winds through a pleasant, younger forest. After rain the path can be muddy, so take care.

WALK 52 WOOLSBARROW HILL FORT
DURATION: *Flexible*
STARTING POINT: *Wareham to Bere Regis road*
FOOD: *The Silent Woman, Coldharbour. Dogs allowed in public bar.*
About halfway between the Silent Woman and the A35 and shortly before you reach the overhead power lines there is a car park on the right. Follow the waymarkers to Woolsbarrow which is the smallest hillfort in south east Dorset. From the summit there are wide views to the far horizons together with pleasant walks along the many paths through the pine forest.

At nearby Sugar Hill on the Wareham to Bere Regis road there is a small white cross by the wayside on the right with the simple inscription '1928'. In that year a car belonging to a family on holiday from Watford was in collision with a tarmac lorry which shed its hot load over their 14 year old daughter. As a result she died horribly from her injuries and to this day the cross is usually well tended by council workmen.

WALK 53 SHERFORD BRIDGE TO STROUD BRIDGE
DURATION: *Flexible*
STARTING POINT: *B3075 car park at Sherford Bridge*
FOOD: *Silent Woman, Coldharbour. Dogs allowed in public bar.*
This walk takes you across a field then past Morden Bog - not at all as unpleasant as its name, it is a site of Special Scientific Interest - across heathland and Wareham Forest. Safe, off the lead walking.

WALK 54 ORGANFORD TO SHERFORD BRIDGE

DURATION: *one and a half miles*
STARTING POINT: *Organford village*
FOOD: *Cock and Bottle, Morden. Dogs welcome.*

Almost opposite Organford Post Office is a bridge over a stream and just beyond that is a track. Follow this for about 100 yards and you will see a footpath sign on the right pointing to Sherford Bridge. The track is hedged and safe for dogs which may scent the occasional rabbit or pheasant. You skirt the edge of Wareham Forest, emerging at Sherford Bridge. If you would like a longer outing, this could be combined with the Sherford Bridge to Stroud Bridge walk (Walk 53).

WALK 55 WAREHAM COMMON

DURATION: *Flexible*
STARTING POINT: *West Walls car park, Wareham*
FOOD: *Antelope Hotel, West Street. Well behaved dogs welcome.*

There are several possible starting places for this walk but I find West Walls car park convenient. The Common is larger than it first appears, following the River Piddle to the east and the railway line and Wareham Bypass to the west. You may encounter cows, so control your dog but there is plenty of space for all.

Take the track at the top end of the car park and keep to the lower path. Emerging on to the Common you may continue under the road flyover and the railway bridge. At least in 1993 the blackberries in September were large and plentiful but I cannot guarantee they will always be so! A mill has been on this site since time immemorial and the house just past the road flyover is a fine example of domestic Georgian architecture. A recommended walk.

WALK 56 SOUTH HAVEN POINT TO CORFE CASTLE

DURATION: *About 6 miles, depending on route taken*
STARTING POINT: *Sandbanks Car Ferry*
FOOD: *Shell Bay Cafe near the Ferry; or Marblers Café or The Greyhound if you reach Corfe Castle! Dogs allowed on a lead in all of these*

A longer walk than most in this book, you simply follow the beautiful western edge of the harbour until you reach a rough track that leads to Greenlands Farm. After that, signposts direct you through Purbeck Forest and Rempstone Heath. Deer can often be seen, shyly hiding in the conifers on this walk. In the main, the paths beyond Greenland Farm are sandy but before that the harbour edges can be boggy so strong footwear is essential. The Oil People have moved into Arne Peninsula and Wytch Farm, so avoid these tracks as vehicles can appear without warning. Otherwise, this is an interesting walk. I have seen a small white egret here in winter, rarely seen on these shores and looking for all the world like a small ghostly heron. I suggest you carry an Ordnance Survey map, in case you miss your way!

WALK 57 WINSPIT

DURATION: *Flexible*
STARTING POINT: *Car park, Worth Matravers*
FOOD: *Puffin Restaurant, Worth Craft Centre. Dogs welcome*

The first short stretch is via roads and 'on the lead'. Head downhill from the car park, past the Square and Compass and the picturesque duckpond in the pretty stone-built village of Worth Matravers. Go down London Row (which couldn't be further from a London scene if it tried!) and follow the waymarked footpath across fields to Seacombe and Winspit. At one time this was a very isolated spot but it is becoming more popular as people discover it. The walk can be extended by following the Coastal Path but watch your dog carefully as there are steep cliffs. Another cautionary note - there may be livestock in the fields, in which case dogs should be on a lead.

WALK 58 ST ALBANS HEAD/PIER BOTTOM

DURATION: *Flexible*
STARTING POINT: *Car park at Renscombe*
FOOD: *Puffins Restaurant, Worth Matravers Craft Centre. Dogs welcome*

St Albans Head extends out into the English Channel with fine views in all directions. Follow the waymarked rough gravel road to the Head where you will see the ancient St Albans Chapel and fantastic scenery on a clear day, especially westwards with Emmetts Hill nearby, then Hounstout, Swyre Head, Gad Cliff and Portland.

An alternative is to turn right from the gravel road just before the quarry and follow the signpost's directions across fields to Pier Bottom. If you want to make this a circular walk you can continue along the coastal path following the signs back to Renscombe, or for an even longer walk, to Chapmans Pool/Renscombe. Beware of steep cliffs though and keep your dog on a lead as an agile rabbit might entice him over the edge - a dreadful thought!

WALK 59 PRIESTS WAY, WORTH MATRAVERS TO SWANAGE

DURATION: *Approximately 4 miles*
STARTING POINT: *Worth Matravers car park*
FOOD: *Puffins Restaurant, Worth Craft Centre. Dogs welcome.*

From the village car park go towards the Square and Compass then turn left past the Craft Centre, keeping to the road. A little way further on your right a waymarked footpath leads across the fields, joining Priests Way near Eastington Farm. As its name implies, this was the ancient track used by priests since Saxon times when visiting the outlying parishes - and also, as rumour has it - by smugglers. Dry stone walls edge much of the Way which can be muddy in places after rain. On this walk you will find old Purbeck stone cottages and farmsteads, invisible from the main road and also field systems unchanged since Saxon times.

WALK 60 POUNDBURY HILL FORT
DURATION: *Flexible*
STARTING POINT: *West end of Poundbury West Industrial Estate*
FOOD: *Cornwall Arms, Alexander Road, Dorchester. Dogs made very welcome*
From the Top-o-Town roundabout in Dorchester take the Bridport road. Immediately before the castle-like Dorset Military Museum turn right into Poundbury Road. After approximately half a mile, opposite Normandy Way you may park in the small rough layby. A stile leads into the grassy area of Poundbury. There was a Roman cemetery here in bygone days, excavated in the 1970's. There are still traces of a Roman aqueduct on the northern side of the hill which carried water into Dorchester from as far away as ten miles.

WALK 61 CASTLE COVE TO FERRYBRIDGE
DURATION: *Approximately one mile*
STARTING POINT: *Old Castle Road to Castle Cove, roadside parking*
FOOD: *Old Castle Inn. Dogs allowed in Clearmount Road entrance bar*
Beyond the modern building overlooking the seashore a track stretches away along the coast towards Portland. If you climb the grassy bank on the sea side of the old railway track (now surfaced with concrete) you will be rewarded by fine views over Portland Harbour and the chalk cliffs of the Dorset Coast. The walk ends at Ferrybridge on the road to Portland. Not very good scenery inland, but seawards it is spectacular.

WALK 62 TOUT QUARRY, PORTLAND
DURATION: *Flexible*
STARTING POINT: *Car park, top of hill overlooking Chesil Beach*
FOOD: *George Hotel, Reforne. Dogs allowed on a lead in public bar*
For a walk that is really different try this one! Cross over the road on the hairpin bend at the top of the steep hill into the Isle of Portland and follow the concrete sign, 'Footpath' pointing left. This will bring you into the quarry and scattered around are some fifty sculptures, carved from the living rock. They crop up in unexpected places adding interest to the walk. There are bunny scents for your dog, but beware, r----t is a forbidden word on Portland where natives truly believe the furry creatures and their burrowing portend ill-luck, and saying 'the word' could produce a landslip or fall of stone!

The views are excellent from high points in the quarry with approximately 15 miles of shingle beach stretching away into the distance. Over the centuries the sea has graded the pebbles, the largest being at Portland and gradually getting smaller towards Burton Bradstock. It is said that fishermen coming ashore on a dark night can tell their position by the size of the stones.

The George Hotel allows dogs in the Kings Shilling bar and is the oldest inhabited building in Portland. Dating back to Jacobean times the Courts Leet used to be held here.

(See also 'Dog permitted attractions - Tout Quarry Sculpture Park and Workshop')

DOG PERMITTED PLACES OF INTEREST

'DOGS DIE IN HOT CARS', so I have tracked down places of interest which your dog can enjoy in your company.

More detailed information, i.e. current opening times and charges are available at Tourism Departments - so DO check before you go.

BLUE POOL

Between Wareham and Swanage, signposted off the A351.

Dogs allowed on a lead. Woodland area surrounding a lake formed by excavation of clay. The water appears blue and is a peaceful haven in summer. There is a café which allows dogs inside (what a rarity!) plus an interesting craft shop. The soda bread from their own bakery is recommended!

CORFE CASTLE

Between Wareham and Swanage on the A351.

One of the few National Trust properties that admits dogs - but they must be on a lead. A lovely ruin in a gap in the Purbeck hills, it was slighted by Cromwell's men following a siege in the Civil War. If you would like to know its Tudor history - read my historical novel, *The Bountifull Gyfte*.

No dogs in the National Trust café unfortunately as it is beautifully situated, but Marbler's café next to the Post Office in West Street make them welcome, as does The Greyhound in the Square.

PUTLAKE ADVENTURE FARM

Langton Matravers on the B3069, bottom end of village.

Dogs allowed on leads but you MUST NOT let them disturb the animals. A lovely place for children with 'hands on' feeding of lambs, kids and calves - and all points of interest are under cover if it rains. There is a walk (leaflet giving details available at the farm) and a picnic area and patio where you can sit with your dog, but they are not allowed in the café.

UPTON COUNTRY PARK

On the A35 within easy reach of Poole and Bournemouth. Admission free.

This is lovely parkland stretching from the road right down to the harbour's edge. Informal and formal gardens are a joy to wander through and admire and there is also a woodland walk to the west. There are trails around the perimeter of the park, partly on board walks over the mudflats. Lead restrictions apply because of the wildfowl which wander freely in the park. The house dates from the early 19th century, built by Christopher Spurrier whose family made their riches from the Newfoundland trade, but it is not generally open to the public. There are nature trails, a visitor centre, picnic sites and a patio café where dogs are permitted.

LANGMOORE MANOR
Near Charmouth at the junction of the A35/A3052 Bridport to Lyme Regis road.
Set in 18 acres of formal gardens, woodland, ponds and fields in which black sheep, pigs and geese graze. Wild areas merge with cultivated, and dogs on leads are welcome. Plants and terracotta pots are on sale and there is a pretty conservatory café where dogs are permitted.

TOUT STONE QUARRY WORKSHOP, PORTLAND
For further information telephone 081 341 6742 or St Georges Centre and Tourist Office, Reforne, Portland.
If you have visited the quarry on Walk 62 and have been inspired to try your hand at sculpting, weekly courses are held here in the workshop. You may be accompanied by your dog, too, I am advised. A holiday course with a difference!

MILTON ABBEY GROUNDS
From the lower end of the village take the road to Hilton and having passed under a bridge you will soon see the entrance to Milton Abbey on your left. Now a public school, the house was once the home of Lord Milton who had the old village demolished in the 18th century so he could have 'peace and solitude' and rebuilt the present village out of sight of his mansion. You may park in the car park (charge) and explore the grounds which are beautiful. The path continues on past a lovely lake with woods on the far side - very peaceful. Dogs are allowed but must be on a lead.

PARK FARM MUSEUM, MILTON ABBAS
On the Stickland/Bulbarrow road and half a mile from the top end of Milton Abbas village.
Suitable for all the family with a love of old things, and your dog is allowed to accompany you on a lead. Here you will find rural bygones, old farm implements, farm animals, tractor and pony rides, milking, a childrens playground and at times a blacksmith. There is a picnic site 600 feet above sea level with fabulous views to the distant coast. In the museum are also documents and photos of old Milton Abbas. Dogs are not allowed in the café but you may take your food outside to the picnic tables.

MOORS VALLEY COUNTRY PARK

Horton Road, Ashley Heath, near Ringwood

Open all year except Christmas day. Car parking charges vary throughout the year. Here you will find quiet walks, Moors Valley railway, a golf centre, waymarked trails and play areas for children. Dogs are allowed off the lead except in Childrens Play Areas, the Golf Centre and near the Visitors Centre. It is requested that dogs do not foul footpaths. Children, adults and dogs can really enjoy themselves here. Allow the best part of day though as there is plenty to see and do. Dogs are not allowed in the café, but they can go on the patio area at the rear where there are picnic tables.

DORSET HEAVY HORSE CENTRE

Brambles Farm, Edmondsham between Verwood and Alderholt.

A lovely day out for the family and your dog although he must be on a lead for his own safety and that of the residents which range from huge Shire horses to miniature ponies. There are daily demonstrations plus a Pets Corner. The Centre has its own gift shop, and a café that permits well-behaved dogs.

OLD WARDOUR CASTLE

Between Shaftesbury and Salisbury, signposted from the A30.

A visit to the castle which is managed by English Heritage could be combined with Walk 46. Dogs are allowed in if they are on a lead and you 'clear up' after them. The 14th century ruins are beautifully situated, surrounded by woods and on the shores of a lake. It was slighted in 1643 in the Civil War. Do not miss the 18th century grotto - a hidey-hole of nooks and alcoves.

EXBURY GARDENS

Two and a half miles south east of Beaulieu.

Two hundred acres of woodland gardens with probably the best display of azaleas and rhododendrons you will see anywhere in the UK. There are also camellias, magnolias and a field of daffodils near the shores of Beaulieu River. Laid out by the Rothschild family the gardens are a feast of colour in spring and early summer. There is also a spectacular rock garden. Dogs are allowed on a lead. A café has tables outside where you may sit with your dog.

RSPCA HAMPSHIRE AND DORSET ANIMAL HOME

Ashley Heath, near Ringwood.

Open Day, last Sunday every July. Many stalls, Exemption Dog Show, displays, pony rides, food, etc. A really good day out for all the family in a worthy cause. Dogs welcome on leads.